if / when

if / *when*

A Poetry Collection by Diana Arnold

© 2022 Diana Arnold. All rights reserved.
This material may not be reproduced in any form, published,
reprinted, recorded, performed, broadcast,
rewritten or redistributed without
the explicit permission of Diana Arnold.
All such actions are strictly prohibited by law.

Cover & Book Art by Becca Line
Cover Design by Shay Culligan

Edited by: Nicholas Canfield

ISBN: 978-1-63980-172-5

Kelsay Books
502 South 1040 East, A-119
American Fork, Utah 84003
Kelsaybooks.com

For *Nick,*
Ludovica, and *Mandana*
who inspired, encouraged, and supported
these poems.

my body
writes into your flesh
the poem
you make of me

Audre Lorde, Recreation

Contents

History	11
Veselka	12
L'Ulivo	13
Note to Self	14
Brokelyn	16
Carpenter	17
Both the Path	18
Verbiage	20
Animal	21
Wraparound	22
Laundry Day	23
Service	25
The Other Duck	26
Tight in the Bud	27
Seasons	28
January	29
Applebee's	30
Monogamy	32
Kumquat	33

Know Thyself	35
Compelled	36
Archaeology	37
Ex-Boyfriend	39
Cart / Horse	40
Double	41
P.O.W.	42
Tourist	43
Sometimes, 1	44
Maritime	47
Your Hands	48
Soon Come	49
Wisdom	50
To Conjure	51
Capture the Flag	52
Symphony	55
Thanksgiving	56
If / When	57
Deluge	58
Golden Moment	59

History

History also interests me,
Just differently.

You know dates
You know facts

You memorized even
A paragraph or two
When you were young
To drop in
Some future
Conversation

But no matter gentleman,
I know feelings.

I know which street corner
Where the light hit your collar
How much salt was on my skin
And which day of the week it was
When you failed me.

I too have a good memory,
It's just for better things.

Your facts are for the public
They are not unique
Anyone can know them
But I —
I am an historian.
I cite the personal.

Haven't you learned yet
That the more specific you get
The more you become universal

Veselka

I miss the old New York,

so I go to Veselka
to get my fix.

Sit
alone at the counter
with my borscht
and listen
to two old school
stand-ups discuss
how
every gentleman
is responsible for
his own
unconscious.

L'Ulivo

Nature,
She knows

It comes
And
It goes

Fits and bursts
Leaps and false starts
Boundaries and firsts

We
Weave
Things
Into
Ourselves

My braids
My Dad
This
New feeling
Of You
In my hands

And if
We are
Lucky at all
We root
Like an olive tree,

and
when
we
are
ripe
we fall.

Note to Self

The morning after
your lover leaves
please, do not
go to New Orleans
by yourself.

The sweat will greet
you something sticky
and it won't be from
sex it is from
the Mississippi
M - I - Double - S
only has 3 letters less
three sounds less
than a symphony

And I promise,
this river will
call to you
at sunset and
beg you to hold
it's crescent city
in your hands
like a trumpet
and bugle your troubles
down into the delta of it

Do not do this.
Stay above water. Keep
your love a secret.

Ladies and gentlemen,
do not go
down to Frenchmen
when you are

thinking about your man,
because the old jazz
standards rearranged
will call you in
and remind you of
the records
your father
used to play,
and
then there will be
two men suddenly
who are not there
and that is
two
too many.

I only want to feel things fully.

(I feel forever
in the beginning
of everything)

Like an old tug boat,
I seem slow
and natural
but
there is much
movement going on
beneath —

I have a lot
of taught roots
but
not a lot of green.

I am in need of watering.

So it seems fitting
that it is storming
in this city.
Two nights in
and there is already
lightening.

Awaking in the night
to loud, low
bass thunder
sounds like an old clarinet—
the rain comes
through the window
onto my cheek

I'm half asleep
and I am wet.

My fingers move toward
the southern part of
my body in search
of warmer climate,
and they have found it.

My lower lip still thick
with the remnants
of humid July kisses
and loosely bitten,
oversalted skin

It gets hot
down south
but nowhere close
to the heat we had
in Brooklyn.

Brokelyn

I can feel broken
then come to Brooklyn
and have an immediate sense
of my own
direction

It isn't easy
but it is East
or it is West
it is North
or
it is South,
it is a grid

Experiences that live
in the corners
and up
    on the curbs

I see my
reflection, undeterred

look down
and scramble to
collect all the
poetry
o
u
r
i
n
g
out
of
my
mouth

Carpenter

Pat me down, partner.
Bring your tools, noble carpenter.

Slide your hands
over my corners.

Smooth
you round them
and add pressure
to remove
my past dust
with your finger

behold—!
my original molding.

Then,
take a
breath in

look me in the eyes
and tell me what

you can build, with
what you are holding.

Both the Path

I am not the end result.

I am a conduit
always have been
I connect

one point or
one chapter to another
one part-of-oneself to the other

I am instrumental in
bringing things together

But, I am never
the final destination.

I am not what one ends up with.

I am but
the wood
atop
the rock
atop
the river
you have
to cross
over
in order to get it

When will I be the thing that someone wants to hold *as* I grow?

Who will walk with me
through the mulch
of my former selves
and plant their wildflowers
along my grass?

How can I
make myself
both, the waterfall
and the path?

Verbiage

Up early
purely
because you
awaken
something in me,

But is that even the right verbiage?

because it's a
part of me
I didn't
even know
was there
to begin with.

Animal

Who,
Other than he?

Animal,
Answer me.

Wraparound

I want a wraparound porch
and a wraparound man
and for trust to wrap around us
while we love each other as best we can.

And I also want a stoop
leading up to some stone
could be brown or could be cobbled
but the building will be tall
and we will call it home.

And I also want a partner
who will take all the pictures
and a family that travels
but kids that call
themselves New Yorkers.

And I also want the country,
crepes with lots and lots of
butter in the mornings
after walks at dawn
with a dog, chopped
firewood and chimneys.

I want so many things.
What wants me?

Laundry Day

I find myself rearranging things
Moving pictures in their frames
Changing the order of my books
Because I've changed.

Old magnetic poetry
Pulled from the fridge
My prized DVD collection
That I never watch
Now in the cupboard
Even though I love it so much
Moving each of my plants
A little to the right tonight -
I am in awe of how they
Always grow towards the light.

I find myself making space

Throwing out blankets, socks
Making space within the space I have.
No real reason really—
Just a shedding feeling

It's new to me
To move laterally
I always start everything
Over completely
But it's so much easier
To just adjust what
I have already.

There is enough space here
For me

And for the *thought* of you, too
That's become clear.

Your memory and me
Have become quite close
Your spirit would have
No problem living here.

My toes,
Underneath the coffee table now
Push back the backgammon set

Slide forward the aged leather
In preparation for a future occasion
When your feet will want to rest there . . .

On a faraway Sunday
Afternoon or some such, when
We are in love.

I imagine you will be relaxed
Put your feet up
Think nothing of it -
But I will smile
To myself because today
I had to make
A little bit of space
So that in the future, you fit.

. . . And that's what
I think about
When my laundry is in
It's 2 a.m.

And I begin to clean
The things I have
Worked so hard in.

Service

It's been so long
I've been a waiter
that now
I get along
better with strangers.

The Other Duck

I look up
at my ducks
and see them   all in a row

Say to
the one
in front

"You look
so calm
on top,
but what's
going on
below?"

Tight in the Bud

Be,
The silence of a smooth hand.

Build,
The foundation for something strong.

Say,
Less in every way you can.

Seek,
The answers from those who have been before.

Gather,
Only more wonder.

Water,
Your rhythm.

Remember,
We flower.

Seasons

I'd like
to be
seen in
all seasons.

January

It gets hotter here
in the winter
than it does anywhere.

The salt on the ground
is enough
I am seasoned perfectly

The cracks in the sidewalk
are the black pepper
and if you
ask me I say
the more, the better

So hold my shaker
in your hands
one more time
and grind me
all over
January.

Applebee's

I am buzzing
With retelling
I don't mean to
But I tear up
When I mention
You.

I swell.

I just do.

But when I do
It feels divine -
Like something pouring
Through me
Just by retelling
Our story,
On Dekalb,
Next to an Applebee's.

I can feel the top of my head opening
To all those golden
Inexplicable, ancient things.

And I'm tied to my heart
So my love pushes
My chest out a little more

I'm standing
So
Tall
And my friends are
Looking at me like
They never have before.

It's a look of awe —

That moment when
Midnight Brooklyn
Corner conversation
Reminds us,
Through our Men
The power of
Women.

Monogamy

The only kind of relationship I want is
the one

where
I don't
always
have to be
the strong
one.

Kumquat

1 December
for 2 weeks
I lived at 1218
Harmony Street
70015, New Orleans.

A doctor often
made house calls
on his bike
to the neighbor
across the street.

That neighbor died,
eventually.
I saw them take his body

While standing beneath
a kumquat tree.
The one in the front
next to the blue chair
on the right.
That day it's shade
of bulbous orange
hanged particularly bright.
Very much like
the ones outside
my grandmother's apartment

Not pre-war, but pre-
adolescent.

We had the bottom
level of a duplex
9367 Olympic
Los Angeles,
California 90211.

And do you know
in all those young
years under
the kumquats
at my grandma's
I only ever ate one?

I remember it distinctly.
I was in a hallway.

9 years old
There was a screen door
I liked it but
sour, was
too hard to eat.
A process -
I remember it not
feeling worth it to me.

I see my hand reach
out now, again
for the strange fruit.

I grasp it,
let go at
the last second

and give thanks for
things still connected to
their roots.

Know Thyself

What is the point
of knowing yourself
if
everyone is only
concerned with
themselves?

Compelled

I am in the light
Or I *am* the light

I can never quite get it right

All I know is that I shine
All I can tell you is
It is my time

And I don't know why
It has taken this long,
But I fit inside myself now
And I am strong

And I have room to let you in some

You, my audience
You, anyone
I do
I've got room

Come over,
I know how good
It feels
To be listened to

But, do
Whatever work
You have to do
On yourself,

So that when
You come
To me
You come,
Compelled.

Archaeology

I'm starting to think
Differently about love.
I'm beginning to think of it
As an uncovering of.
Like, archaeology
I am dusty
You must use
Your hands
For me.

And it's not a one-time thing, discovery
It's best when its constant
When it keeps happening
And it doesn't always have
To be something new
I imagine actually the very best feeling
Might be discovering something
Again and again and again
That I already knew.

I think that word
Is familiar
And I think that's probably what
Makes a family
Like you would feel
Learned to me,
Like a grammar rule
That doesn't quite make sense
But when you use it right
The letters do somehow
Look better together.

And you,
Whoever you are,
Whoever you are on your way to becoming

As you are coming to me
Will know something
And that is that
Someone knows you
And that someone will be me.

And like every good rule
There is always an exception,
But we will be it.

We will wrap ourselves in language
Rearrange our limbs like letters
Masculine and feminine
Gerund endings written
In the air together
Like a 7th grader
At a spelling bee
I will write your entire self
On the palm of my hand, invisibly

And look at you
From all angles
Carefully,
Like an I before an E

I know your meaning.

Use you in a sentence
Then announce that
You make perfect
S-e-n-s-e to me.

Ex-Boyfriend

He gives me
a compliment
and I think ugh,
what an idiot.

Cart / Horse

There is just a little
bit of lipstick
on my toothbrush
because I mostly
get ready in a rush

and I mean
to
tell myself not
to
every time
but I always end
up putting my
lipstick on first.

When it comes to you,
I put the cart before the horse.

Double

What a day!

I worked a double
and had to ask some guy
if he still likes me.

He said yes,
and I made four hundred dollars,
so I guess that's something.

P.O.W.

You feel like a solider away at war
And I am proud to think about
What you will lose,
What you will win, and
What you have been fighting for

But there is a romantic woman in me
That also longs to see
You tap on the glass
Take off the strap of
Your army bag and
Kiss me as I open
The front door

Tourist

When I see tourists
Walking in New York
It's just the best!

They are
in Wonder
and Astonishment
always looking up —

I wanna run right up
And say "Hey,

I've lived in New York
For 20 years and I still
Look at her that way."

Sometimes, I

Sometimes I'm direct
And sometimes I'm not
Sometimes I like to listen
And other times I really like to talk
Sometimes I'm quick and
Hard and sometimes
Like when I trust
I get really quiet and soft
Sometimes, I want to let loose
And sometimes I wanna get lost.
And on very few occasions
I like to let it all go
And rest my head
In your lap
Like a cat
And for a moment
Not actually have a single thought
I think about how much I'd
Like to be able
To be weak, a lot
Sometimes I really think love
Is being able to give everything
I can never risk giving up, up

Sometimes I'm flooding
And it's indicative of something
And sometimes I'm stalled
You cannot start me up
Sometimes I turn a corner
And my breath gets short
Because I am absolutely in awe
With so much of this city

With so much of the light

On so many of the sides
Of so many of the buildings
Sometimes it overcomes me
And sometimes I
Don't leave my house
Sometimes I'm empty
Sometimes I'm walking
Down, straight, right, across
Sometimes Brooklyn is my Walden
Sometimes I'm my own Whitman
And then sometimes I despise the very
Walls that this city has
Encased me in

Sometimes I think
Everything happens for a reason
And sometimes I spend my time
Feeling like a victim
I'm doing the best that I can
I am
Sometimes I want a partner
And sometimes I just want a man
Most of the time I want
To feel held and like I don't have
To hold anything back
I hate that
I hate having to do that

Sometimes, I write poems
And sometimes I don't
Sometimes you read them
When you're interested
Or when you need them
And sometimes you don't

Right now our bodies
Are in deep,
Deep, conversation
So you've no urge
Now for reading
Of course not
Nothing new is being written

But you will immediately
Be able to feel again
When it is -
When a poem comes
You will feel it
Because you are
The very thing
That elicits it

Sometimes, I
Fall in love
In an instant

And sometimes
It takes me
So so long,
I
drip
it.

And sometimes, I
think I know exactly,
exactly what I want -

But sometimes, I
don't.

Maritime

I want our love to heal us both
                            both.

Is that asking too much?
                much

I want us to be the water the oars the air the foam
the salt thegravitationalpullofitall the moon
the sun the sailor and also the boat

 It takes us being all
                            all
of those for
our love
to float.

Your Hands

Whenever
I have any
moment of doubt

I think about
your hands.

They grab me —
make me
not worry.

Finally,
hands that are strong enough to hold me.

Soon Come

So I say come.

Come.
Come to me.
Come to me poetry
Come to me money
Come to me whoever you are as you are becoming
Come to me career
Come to me prayer
Come to me mother
Come to me nature
Come to me moment
Come to me spirit
Come to me, useless.

I have to come to it.

Wisdom

I can use my gifts
on myself.

In fact,
I must.

To Conjure

I have the power
to conjure.

Yes, create something from nothing

I can write a poem
and summon you here
with me on my couch.

Yes, I do that now

I bring people
to me with
my mouth.

Capture the Flag

I swear,
I was born
in the wrong decade.

I just wanna scat
and wear black
and smoke
and listen to jazz
and ride the trains and
watch the people and
walk the streets.
I am of the spirit
of the beats,
I think

And our love feels no different
It has a classic, slightly
revolutionary feel to it
Our love makes us take it to the streets

You climb the cobblestone
staircases of foreign cities
when you need to think about
how to shape your own world.
Is it a mountain from
where you are now, your future?
And if so, is there a part of you
that feels excited and inspired by that?

I take it to the avenues.
They are longer and wider
I find my thoughts
get more space there

And every time I bump into someone

or want to take a sharp corner
I remember to keep my eyes up—
I have never been someone
who looks down as they walk

I love the lines of this city too.
They're straight. They're sharp.
They get you to where you're going.
There's no denying it, they work!

Down Fifth, up Seventh
Streets just waiting for
me, since 17
Actually since before that
since I first watched
When Harry Met Sally,
the arch in that
Washington Square Park
did something to me

Led me towards every single thing

And you were here
all the time too.

Uptown, with other
beacons that guided you
Tell me, have we walked
past each other
on Columbus before?

While we were both doing
everything we could to
become who we are
right now?

Right now,
I write at night
because after work
I'm up.

And it's just so important to
write things down
before tomorrow comes,

because when it does
everything might be different.

But at least I have
yesterday's record of it

when it wasn't.

*

As you travel
you see what makes
a great city -
it's history.

So come, explorer
enter my gates

sweat in my streets

cool yourself in
my holy cathedral

and then,
plant your flag in me.

Symphony

I am getting lucky.

The winds have changed,
good things are coming

And just as music is made
from the notes that are
not played
so too, are we

We, built of the in between

Kindred spirits who have never really
had to choose anything
because we have always been
in control of everything

But, our time is coming

And I am faithful
that my doing nothing
is actually a symphony
coming

Thanksgiving

It's Thursday,
the air is cold
the sky is blue
the church bells are ringing
and I am moved—

reminded of Edgar Allen Poe
because my bells bells bells
are ringing too.

Take a left,
down the subway steps
and there to meet me
like destiny
a young man singing
Leonard Cohen's Hallelujah
on Thanksgiving.

Bells and prayers score me this morning.

I stop
I listen
I decide
there are
no such things
as coincidences.

We see what we feel,
we reflect our own environments.

My hips pinch
with a flash
of the night before
and I think to myself,
there is much
to be thankful for.

If / When

The change in me
is the change in him.

I see so much more
when I am not looking.

Deluge

What comes
After you
Get unstuck?

A flood.
A flood comes.
It does.

It must.

New focus,
New partner,
Defer to your center,
Re-enter,
And trust:

The rush, was all us.

Golden Moment

I know love.

Which is to say,
I hold it

with both hands
above my head
like a golden orb
and I offer it up
to my ancestors
to show them
what has grown
since they have
lived.

About the Author

Diana Arnold is a New York City poet, playwright, and performer. She is committed to creating original and autobiographical work that lifts her audience up and speaks to the connectedness of all things.

After arriving in New York City in 2002, she now writes from her dream home in Brooklyn. You can discover her short film, audiobook, and all other work at onthetablenyc.com

www.ingramcontent.com/pod-product-compliance
Lightning Source LLC
Chambersburg PA
CBHW071013160426
43193CB00012B/2034